Primer Level / Level One
(Prep / Grade 1)

CLASSIC MELODIES from GREAT OPERAS

For Piano
for beginners of all ages

compiled and arranged by
John W. Schaum

New Editing and Revised Arrangements by Wesley Schaum

Foreword

This series helps develop music appreciation early in a student's piano study. The books are appropriate for adults and children. Very easy arrangements enable the student to play famous melodies by the world's great composers.

Duet accompaniments are included for each melody. The ensemble experience provides valuable rhythmic training and makes the music sound more complete.

Other albums in this series are:

- Classic Melodies from GREAT BALLETS
  Themes, illustrations and stories from 20 famous ballets
- Classic Melodies from GREAT COMPOSERS
  Famous themes by 20 master composers from Bach to Bartok
- Classic Melodies from GREAT SYMPHONIES
  Excerpts from 20 symphonies; gummed instrument picture stamps

SCHAUM PUBLICATIONS, INC.
10235 N. Port Washington Rd. • Mequon, WI • 53092
www.schaumpiano.net

07-43
M-11

Index

Puccini, Giacomo (1858-1924)

Madam Butterfly

"One Fine Day" from Act II

Cio-Cio San (Cho Cho San), a Japanese girl, known as Madam Butterfly, marries Lt. Pinkerton of the U.S. Navy. Pinkerton leaves Cio-Cio San, but promises to return. One day she sees his boat in the harbor and happily sings "One Fine Day." Unknown to Cio-Cio San, Pinkerton has his American wife with him. On learning this, Cio-Cio San takes her own life.

place Madam Butterfly stamp here

Andante

Duet Accompaniment

Notes with stems UP are to be played with the *right* hand. Notes with stems DOWN are to be played with the *left* hand.

Bizet, Georges (1838-1875)

Carmen

"Toreador Song" from Act II

Carmen, a flirtatious Spanish gypsy girl, has made Don Jose, a soldier, desert the army. Tiring of him, she leaves him for Escamillo, a toreador. Escamillo sings the "Toreador Song," in which he tells of the dangers and excitement of the bullring. Don Jose, jealous because Carmen loves Escamillo, kills her at the bullring entrance.

place Carmen stamp here

Tempo di Marcia (see footnote)

Duet Accompaniment

Teacher's Note: The dotted quarter + 8th note rhythm may be taught by rote. If the pupil has not yet had fractions in school, the explanation of this rhythm can be delayed until the student is more advanced.

Verdi, Giuseppe (1813-1901)

Rigoletto

"Ladies Are Frivolous" from Act IV

In the Duke of Mantua's court, a hunchback jester, Rigoletto, is thought to be in love with a beautiful girl. However, this girl is Rigoletto's daughter, Gilda. The Duke, disguised as a student, has charmed Gilda into loving him. Hoping to reveal the duke's frivolous nature, Rigoletto takes Gilda to an inn where they see the duke lightheartedly sing "Ladies Are Frivolous." Rigoletto's plan to have the duke assassinated misfires, and Gilda is killed instead. Rigoletto dies from shock and grief.

place
Rigoletto
stamp here

Duet Accompaniment

Puccini, Giacomo (1858-1924)

La Boheme

"Musetta's Waltz" from Act II

La Boheme is the story of four Bohemians who live together is a Paris attic. One, Rudolfo, is in love with Mimi, who is seriously ill. Another, Marcello, has quarreled with his former sweetheart, Musetta. Musetta flirts with Marcello as she sings "Musetta's Waltz" in a cafe. Marcello is unable to resist her and they are reunited. Rudolfo and Mimi are not so fortunate because Mimi dies.

place
La Boheme
stamp here

Moderato (see footnote)

Duet Accompaniment

Teacher's Note: Rhythms involving the single 8th note and 8th rest may be taught by rote. If the pupil has not yet had fractions in school, the explanation of this rhythm can be delayed until the student is more advanced.

Verdi, Giuseppe (1813-1901)

Aida

"Heavenly Aida" from Act I

Rhadames, an Egyptian guard, is secretly in love with Aida, an Ethiopian princess who is a slave at the Egyptian court. While thinking of Aida, Rhadames sings of his love for her in "Heavenly Aida." To aid her captured father, Aida questions Rhadames about military matters. Her father hides and listens, but is discovered. Rhadames then is condemned to be buried alive. Aida decides to join him and they perish together.

place
Aida
stamp here

Andantino

Duet Accompaniment

Puccini, Giacomo (1858-1924)

Tosca

"The Stars Were Shining" from Act III

In 19th century Rome, Mario is in prison for hiding a political fugitive. Tosca is in love with Mario and hopes to free him. Scarpia, the evil police chief, uses threats and deceit to learn the hiding place of the fugitive. Tosca kills Scarpia for revenge. Mario, facing execution, sings a farewell song, "The Stars Were Shining." After his death, Tosca kills herself.

place
Tosca
stamp here

Duet Accompaniment

Verdi, Giuseppe (1813-1901)

La Traviata

"Ever Free" from Act I

Violetta, a happy, carefree girl, falls in love with Alfredo Germont. Enchanted with her new love, she sings a dazzling song, "Ever Free." Alfredo's father asks Violetta to give up his son for his family's honor. Violetta does so. Unaware of the sacrifice, Alfredo denounces her publicly. Too late, Alfredo learns the truth as Violetta dies in his arms.

place
La Traviata
stamp here

Duet Accompaniment

Verdi, Giuseppe (1813-1901)

Il Trovatore

"Anvil Chorus" from Act II

Manrico, a troubadour, and Count Luna fight a duel over the love of Leonora. Wounded, Manrico is nursed at a gypsy camp by Azucena. While the other gypsies work vigorously swinging their hammers at the forges, and lustily singing the "Anvil Chorus," Manrico and Azucena plot revenge against the count. However, both are caught and sentenced to die. Leonora drinks poison for revenge against the count.

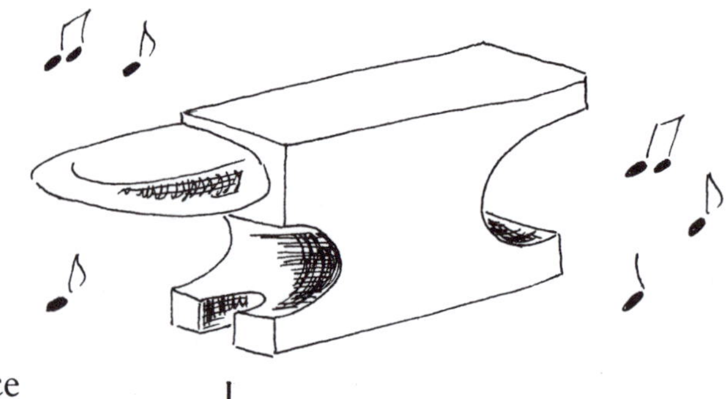

place
Il Trovatore
stamp here

Andantino (see footnote)

Duet Accompaniment

Teacher's Note: The dotted quarter + 8th note rhythm may be taught by rote. If the pupil has not yet had fractions in school, the explanation of this rhythm can be delayed until the student is more advanced.

Mascagni, Pietro (1863-1945)

Cavalleria Rusticana

"Intermezzo" from Act I

A Sicilian girl, Santuzza, is rejected by her lover Turiddu, who turns to his former sweetheart, Lola. Santuzza, wanting revenge, tells Lola's husband, Alfio, of his wife's unfaithfulness. While Turiddu and the villagers attend Easter services in church, this famous "Intermezzo" hymn is played. After church, Alfio challenges Turiddu to a duel in which Turiddu is killed.

place Cavalleria Rusticana stamp here

Duet Accompaniment

Gounod, Charles (1818-1893)

Faust

"Soldiers' Chorus" from Act IV

Faust, an aged philosopher, desiring to recapture his youth, sells his soul to the "Evil One," Mephistopheles, who fulfills the wish. Faust courts Marguerite while her brother, Valentine, is away with the army. The returning victorious soldiers sing the "Soldiers' Chorus." Learning that Marguerite has been abandoned by Faust, Valentine challenges him to a duel. Marguerite, overcome with remorse, dies and ascends to heaven, while Faust is dragged into the underworld.

place
Faust
stamp here

Duet Accompaniment

Leoncavallo, Ruggiero (1858-1919)

Pagliacci

"On With The Show" from Act I

Pagliacci (a name which means comedy players) tells the story of the loves and intrigues of a group of strolling players. Canio, head of these players, sings "On With the Show" at the end of the first act.

place
Pagliacci
stamp here

Lento

Duet Accompaniment

Mozart, Wolfgang Amadeus (1756-1791)

Marriage of Figaro

"If You Want To Dance" from Act I

Count Almaviva flirts with Susanna, maid to the Countess – but Susanna and Figaro (the Count's valet) are in love. The Count arranges to meet Susanna in the garden. Hearing of this, the Countess sends a page-boy, dressed in Susanna's clothes, to this meeting. Figaro and Susanna are also in the garden. The Count sees them and thinks Susanna is his wife. Subsequently, the true identity of each lady is revealed, and the opera ends on a merry note as they all go to celebrate the marriage of Figaro. Figaro sings "If You Want to Dance."

place Marriage of Figaro stamp here

Allegretto

Duet Accompaniment

Rossini, Gioacchino (1792-1868)

Barber of Seville

"Room for the Factotum" from Act I

Figaro, a barber and factotum (jack-of-all-trades), happily sings "Room for the Factotum," a song describing his carefree life. Count Almaviva, in love with Rosina, engages Figaro's services in making arrangements to meet her. Dr. Bartolo, guardian of Rosina, also wants her, but only for her fortune. With Figaro's help, the count meets Rosina. Dr. Bartolo gives his blessing to the marriage when the count gives Rosina's fortune to him.

place Barber of Seville stamp here

Duet Accompaniment

Mozart, Wolfgang Amadeus (1756-1791)

Don Giovanni

"Minuet" from Act I

Don Giovanni is challenged to a duel by the father (Commandant) of a girl he has pursued. The Commandant is killed. Fearing reprisal, Don Giovanni returns to his palace where the peasants are dancing to the music of the famous "Minuet," to celebrate a wedding. At this point, the statue of the Commandant comes to life and orders Don Giovanni to repent. He refuses. The statue disappears, and Don Giovanni is swallowed up by fire.

place Don Giovanni stamp here

Duet Accompaniment

Wagner, Richard (1813-1883)

Die Meistersinger

"Dance of the Apprentices" from Act III

A Meistersinger was a master in the musicians' guild of the 14th century. A young knight, Walther, has fallen in love with Eva. Her father, however, has promised her to the man who wins the Meistersingers' song contest. On the day of the contest, the Meistersingers arrive in great pomp, while the young tradesmen and girls dance to a rustic tune, "Dance of the Apprentices." Walther wins both the contest and Eva.

place
Die
Meistersinger
stamp here

Duet Accompaniment

Verdi, Giuseppe (1813-1901)

The Masked Ball

"I Shall See Her Again" from Act I

Riccardo, King of Sweden, is inspecting the guest list for a masked ball. Included on this list is Amelia, wife of his trusted secretary, Renato. The king and Amelia are secretly in love. In anticipation of seeing her, the king sings, "I Shall See Her Again." At the ball, Renato, learning of his wife's unfaithfulness, kills the king.

place
The Masked Ball
stamp here

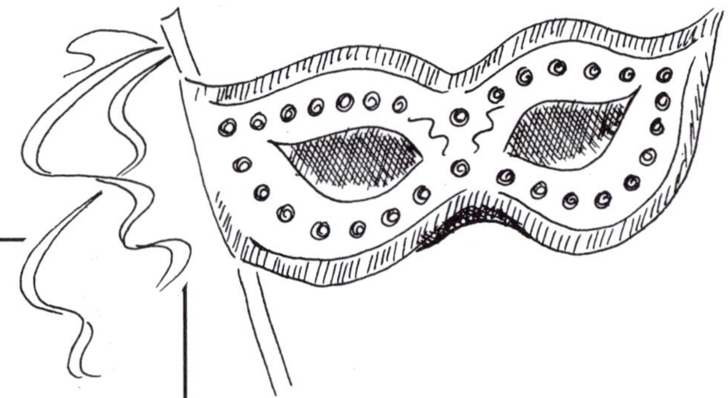

Duet Accompaniment

Wagner, Richard (1813-1883)

Tannhauser

"Pilgrims' Chorus" from Act II

Tannhauser, homesick for life on earth, returns from the underworld to Wartburg (Germany), where his love, Elizabeth, has been waiting for him. In a song contest, Elizabeth's hand in marriage has been promised to the winner. Tannhauser is disgraced when he sings of his love in the underworld. Seeking redemption from his sin, he leaves and joins a group on a pilgrimage, singing the "Pilgrims' Chorus." Saddened during his long absence, Elizabeth becomes ill and dies. When Tannhauser returns, he dies of grief, not knowing that he has miraculously been forgiven.

place Tannhauser stamp here

Andantino

Duet Accompaniment

Verdi, Giuseppe (1813-1901)

The Force of Destiny

"O Thou Heavenly One" from Act III

Don Alvaro, a young prince, and Donna Leonora, daughter of a nobleman, plan to elope. The nobleman is accidentally killed by Alvaro. Don Carlo, the nobleman's son, swears vengeance. Leonora finds refuge in a mountain convent. Alvaro joins the army, and while musing over his past life, he sings "O Thou Heavenly One." This opera ends in tragedy with Alvaro, Carlo and Leonora dead.

place The Force of Destiny stamp here

Duet Accompaniment

Wagner, Richard (1813-1883)

Lohengrin

"Bridal Chorus" from Act III

Elsa has been falsely accused of murdering her brother, Gottfried, who has disappeared. To defend her innocence, a mysterious knight, Lohengrin, arrives. Lohengrin successfully defends Elsa and they make plans to marry. The familiar "Bridal Chorus" is sung at this point. Breaking her promise, Elsa asks the secret identity of Lohengrin, who reveals that he is a Knight of the Holy Grail. As a penalty, Lohengrin must leave, but he enables Gottfried to return. Elsa dies in her brother's arms.

place Lohengrin stamp here

Duet Accompaniment

Humperdinck, Engelbert (1854-1921)

Hansel and Gretel

"There Stands a Little Man" from Act II

Hansel and Gretel happily wander in the woods looking for strawberries. They sing "There Stands a Little Man." Eventually, they come across a house made of gingerbread and decorated with candies. They are invited inside by a witch. With a magic wand, the witch locks up Hansel. Gretel steals the wand, frees Hansel, and they push the witch into an oven where she becomes a gingerbread cake. In case you haven't guessed, the "Little Man" in the song is a mushroom or a jack-in-the-pulpit (flower).

place
Hansel and
Gretel
stamp here

Duet Accompaniment

f order. Name each theme
ɔhengrin" by Wagner

e Masked Ball
nnhauser
e Force of Destiny
hengrin
ınsel and Gretel

Stamps for

GREAT OPERAS

These stamps provide scenes that are symbolic of the opera. After you learn to play each melody, paste the correct stamp in the space provided.

• *The Masked Ball* •

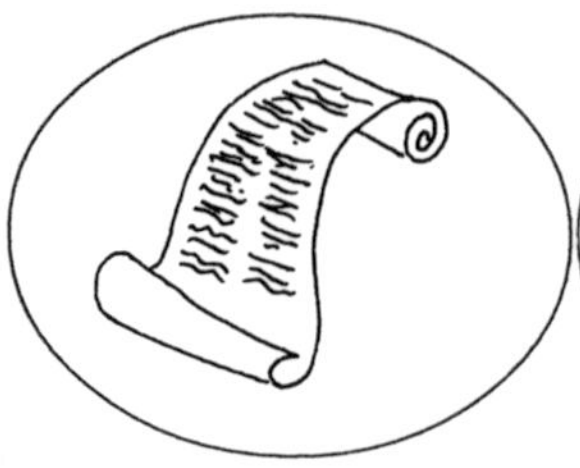

• *Pagliacci* •

• *Tosca* •

• *Madam Butterfly* •

• *Tannhauser* •

• *Marriage of Figaro* •

• *La Traviata* •

• *Carmen* •

• *The Force of Destiny* •

• *Barber of Seville* •

• *Il Trovatore* •

• *Rigoletto* •

• *Lohengrin* •

• *Don Giovanni* •

• *Cavalleria Rusticana* •

• *La Boheme* •

• *Hansel & Gretel* •

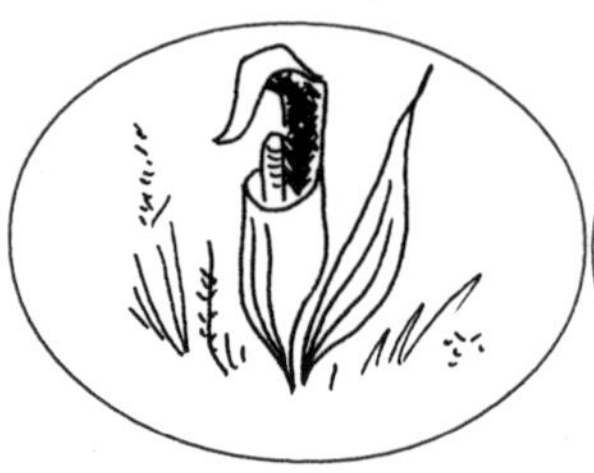

• *Die Meistersinger* •

• *Faust* •

• *Aida* •

NOTE: Some teachers may prefer to remove the stamps from the book and keep them in the studio or home, giving the student each stamp as earned.
Student's Name: ______________________________

Schaum Publications, Inc.
10235 N. Port Washington Rd. • Mequon, WI 53092 • www.schaumpiano.net

him/her identify them. The

Successful Schaum Sheet Music

This is a Partial List — Showing Primer Level through Level 1

✋= 5 Finger Position * = Big Notes • = Original Form ✓ = Chord Symbols

ACTION SOLOS

No.		Title	Composer	LEVEL
52-07	* •	ASTRONAUT ADVENTURE (Left Hand Melody)	*Schaum*	1
52-25	* •	BUBBLE BLUES	*Weston*	1
50-06	* •	SPACE WALK	*Schaum*	P

ANIMALS and BIRDS

No.		Title	Composer	Level
50-12	* •	BIRD CHORUS ✋	*McCullen*	P
52-16	* •	BUSY WOODPECKER ✋ (Staccato)	*Cahn*	1
52-29	•	BUZZY AND WUZZY (Two Kittens)	*Maier*	1
50-15	* •	COPY CAT	*Holmes*	P
52-36	•	DINOSAUR LAND	*Schaum*	1
52-38	•	KANGAROO HOP ✋	*Polk*	1
50-05	* •	PENGUINS AT PLAY ✋	*Heim*	P
52-24	* •	PERKY TURKEY	*Weston*	1
50-04	* •	PLAYFUL POODLE ✋ (Left Hand Melody)	*Schmidt*	P
50-02	* •	PREPOSTEROUS RHINOCEROS	*Schaum*	P
50-11	* •	PUPPY LOVE ✋	*Sprengeler*	P

BOTH HANDS in TREBLE CLEF

No.		Title	Composer	Level
52-27	•	JOYOUS BELLS ✋ (with Duet Accompaniment)	*Cahn*	1

CHRISTMAS

No.		Title	Composer	Level
70-12	*	CHRISTMAS TREE MEDLEY ✋	*Traditional*	P
70-10	*	IT CAME UPON THE MIDNIGHT CLEAR	*Traditional*	1
81-06		LITTLE DRUMMER BOY, The	*Arr. Schaum*	1
70-02		TWELVE DAYS of CHRISTMAS	*All 12 Verses*	1
70-01	*	WHAT CHILD IS THIS? ("Greensleeves")	*Traditional*	1

CIRCUS

No.		Title	Composer	Level
50-10	* •	JALOPY RIDE at the FAIR ✋	*Schaum*	P

CLASSICS

No.		Composer	Title	Level
52-09	*	*Beethoven*	SONG of JOY ("Ode To Joy" from 9th Symph.)	1
52-12	✓	*Handel*	HALLELUJAH CHORUS (Easy Edition)	1
52-37		*Grieg*	IN the HALL of the MOUNTAIN KING	1
52-35		*Rossini*	WILLIAM TELL MARCH	1

COUNTRY/WESTERN

No.		Title	Composer	Level
52-06	* •	PONY RIDE ✋	*McCreary*	1
50-08	* •	TOMAHAWK DANCE ✋ (Minor Key)	*Payne*	P

DESCRIPTIVE MUSIC

No.		Title	Composer	Level
52-39	•	ANCIENT PAGODA	*Biel*	1
50-18	•	AT THE PLAYGROUND ✋	*Revezoulis*	P
52-43	* •	BE A STAR ✋	*King*	1
52-17	* •	CHARM BRACELET	*Cahn*	1
52-32	* •	GLIDING ON THE WIND	*Hampton*	1
52-44	* •	GOING BY, MERRILY	*Rita*	1
50-16	* •	HAPPY SONG ✋	*Leach*	P
52-42	* •	IT'S FUN TO LEARN ✋	*Rita*	1
52-40	•	JOLLY LEPRECHAUN	*Revezoulis*	1
52-14	* •	SLUMBER PARTY	*Stecker*	1
50-17	•	WHISTLING ALONG (w/Duet Accompaniment)	*Cahn*	P
50-14	* •	WINDMILLS ✋	*Russell*	P

DUETS (1 Piano, 4 Hands)

No.		Title	Composer	LEVEL
52-27	•	JOYOUS BELLS ✋ (may also be played as solo)	*Cahn*	1
71-02		PARADE of the TOY SOLDIERS	*Jessel*	1
50-17	•	WHISTLING ALONG (may also be played as solo)	*Cahn*	P

ETHNIC MUSIC

No.		Title	Composer	Level
50-21	•	DUTCH DANCE	*Revezoulis*	P

FOOD

No.		Title	Composer	Level
50-01	* •	BUBBLE GUM ✋(Staccato)	*McCullen*	P
50-03	* •	LOLLIPOP WALTZ ✋	*Schaum*	P
50-09	*	SCRAMBLED EGGS ✋	*Schmidt*	P

HALLOWEEN

No.		Title	Composer	Level
50-19	* •	EVERY WITCH WAY	*Revezoulis*	P
50-20	* •	HALLOWEEN SURPRISE	*Revezoulis*	P
52-15	* •	SPOOK HOUSE (Left Hand Melody)	*Schaum*	1
52-20	* •	SPUNKY SPOOKS (Both Hands in Bass)	*Weston*	1

LEFT HAND MELODY

No.		Title	Composer	Level
52-22	•	KNOCKING AT MY DOOR ✋	*Schaum*	1

MARCHES

No.		Title	Composer	Level
52-34	•	FANFARE	*King*	1

MINOR KEY

No.		Title	Composer	Level
52-28	•	SECRET AGENT	*Weston*	1

OLDIES but GOODIES

No.		Title	Composer	Level
52-21	✓	SCHOOL DAYS	*Edwards*	1

SPORTS/GAMES

No.		Title	Composer	Level
50-07	* •	BIKE HIKE✋	*Schaum*	1
52-10	* •	CHEERLEADER	*Plank*	1
52-18	* •	JOGGING TRAIL ✋ (Minor Key)	*Payne*	1
52-41	•	SKI TRAILS	*King*	1
50-22	* •	TICK TACK TOE ✋	*Revazoulis*	P

SPRINGTIME

No.		Title	Composer	Level
52-04	*	SPRING, SWEET SPRING	*Lincke*	1
52-31	* •	TREES IN THE BREEZE	*Hampton*	1

STACCATO

No.		Title	Composer	Level
52-33	•	HOPSCOTCH	*Hampton*	1
52-11	* •	WINDSHIELD WIPER ROCK (Staccato)	*Noblitt*	1

THANKSGIVING

No.		Title	Composer	Level
52-24	* •	PERKY TURKEY	*Weston*	1

WALTZES

No.		Title	Composer	Level
52-30	•	OPUS ONE	*Cahn*	1